THE GRIEVIN

ALL IN & OUT OF CHURCH

BY:MISS ANNEMARIE E. WEDDERBURN

TABLE OF CONTENTS

IN MEMORY OF

MRS THELMA AGATHA

DRECKETT GREEN

SUNRISE: - 09/07/1937 to SUNSET: -
22/01/2015

A:- DAUGTHER, SISTER, AUNT, COUSIN,
MOTHER, ADOPTIVE MOM, SECOND
MOM, SPIRITUAL MOM, MOTHER-IN-

LAW, SISTER-IN-LAW, GRAND-MOTHER, GOD-MOTHER, WORK COLLEAGUE, CHURCH SISTER, SUNDAY SCHOOL TEACHER, FLOWER ARRANGER, CHOIR MEMBER, ROLE MODEL, ADVISOR, BOSS, SUPERVISIOR, MANAGER AND FRIEND.

WAS A VERY BLESSED WOMAN OF GOD IN FACT AND DEED.

SHE HAD TOUCHED THE LIVES OF MANY IN A GREATLY ALONG WITH MIGTHY POWERFUL WAY.

LEFT HER MARK AND IMPRINT IN THE WORLD OF TODAY.

GONE NOW BUT IN NO WAY IS SHE NOW FORGOTTEN BY THOSE SHE LEFT BEHIND.

DEDICATION

I would like to thank a minister at my church named Reverend Noel Brown for encouraging me to write my book on grief with the unwanted and repeated bad words from both none and current church members on how I was choosing to grieve the unexpected death of my second mom.

I had texted him on and off about all the BRAINLESS, TACTLESS, CLUELESS AND BAD THINGS that folks kept on saying to me that was doing me more HARM than good overall on hearing. The comments left me deeply hurt and steaming mad, so much so that I *decided that I was going to write a book later on the topic of grief for those not in the know of what not to do and SAY.*

Reverend Noel Brown told me "why wait and to get started on writing my grief book now whilst it's all still new and fresh in my mind". He advised me to mention how the unhelpful and discouraging words did make me feel. I eventually listened to his advice. This is my book on grief.

Thanks Uncle Noel for the encouragement to write this book on grief, I do appreciate it.

THE GRIEVING PROCESS

I begin with the grieving process both in and out of church that is paramount the lives that we all live and lead in the world of today. We got two appointments in life that we all can never ever escape.

A time to be born and a time to die just as we all are told and heard from many other in our lives for many years now. We are not in control of when either of these two events does indeed happen all both to and with us. It is something that is indeed out of our hands.

We all definitely can't delay, stall, postpone, fore go and talk our way out of either eventuality. When our time is up it is up. That is all why it is best to live right with everybody no matter whether the person is your relative or friend.

Tomorrow is not promised. I repeat again folk that tomorrow is not promised. If you have to make peace with someone make it or if you owe someone an apology then humble yourself and do it.

Do not at all wait until that person dies and then you are left with a whole pile of what ifs, maybes, couldas, shoulda dones and so ons in the aftermath of it all.

Do go and fix what needs fixing and sorting out with the person and persons today whether a family member or a friend. BELIEVE me you will feel tens time better indeed when you do IT and SO.

I learned a lot from the unexpected death this year of my second mom. Questions that we all should be thinking of, asking and about at both sad and bad time like this. Do you have a will done up already? If NOT please do up a will both NOW and today it help your devastated relatives that is left behind.

Do not wait, delay and stall on your will.DO ONE TODAY. Once you do one up *MAKE SURE* to register it at the national register of wills website *IN CASE* you forget to show it to other in your home or become too incapacitated to point to where it all is kept too.

Do you have a funeral plan already in place? If *NOT* get one in place now and *TODAY* for will do well. Have you brought your grave plait for burial already? If you *HAVE NOT* got one then do one up both now and *TODAY*. Don't delay.

Plan and think ahead. It does help indeed your devastated left behind relatives in deep grief to deal with what you want and don't want at *funeral and other things like estate if that's all in PLACE.*

If your will somewhere in your house tell the executor or law firm that done up the will where it so be if you don't want to tell your family where it all is. This is to ensure that your WISHES not those left behind get done when it comes to who is to get what of your estate.

Recently a lady who WAS my second mom died UNEXPECTEDLY along with very SUDDENLY on me. I REALISED all really very quickly and fastly to how very CLUELESS, TACTLESS HEARTLESS and BRAINLESS people in and out of church can really on so to BE indeed.

People can be OUT OF ORDER. Repetitive comments to me from her DEATH to BURIAL and even up to NOW were all in BAD TASTE and left A LOT TO BE DESIRED with me. Folk did say to me of they think that I'm GRIEVING to hard and long for my dead second mum.

My second mom had only just died on the 22 of January 2015 and was just then only buried on the 25 of February 2015. It is early days STILL. It is FRESH AND NEW still. It is not a crime to SHOW grief by crying.

Folk need to back off, stand down and quite frankly mind their own business. It is as simple as that. MY

THING will always be 'if you do not got anything good and encouraging to say at all TO A SEVERELY GRIEVING PERSON then do folk a favour that are INDEED grieving by just SIMPLY keeping your mouth shot and saying nothing at all.

CLUELESS, TACTLESS, HEARTLESS AND BRAINLESS comments to someone GRIEVING the very SUDDEN or UNEXPECTED loss of either a relative or friend does MORE HARM than good to the person UNFORTUNATE enough to be HEARING it. IT'S NOT EVERYTHING that you think to say to a GRIEVING person that you MUST DO SAY.

THINK PEOPLE THINK. For myself personally, when other suffer the loss of a loved one, the first thing that I do, is go and buy a sympathy card and put in the person door or give person the card straight into their hands.

Depending on who has died and the relationship I had with the person that died, I offer help in going through their belongings and even offer to be of help at the funeral.

There is power in the mouth and tongue. Individuals do WELL to think CAREFULLY about what they say AS spoken HURTFUL words can SEND GRIEVING FOLKS to the breaking point IN both fact and deed too.

In cards I have the tendency to write to person that 'no death is easy to take and handle whether person gone was a relative or friend, healthy or sick, male or female and that HOW I know that the person pain, grief, sorrow and upset is SEVERE'.

I also send 'prayers to the families' in the days and weeks ahead planning the funeral, day of the funeral itself and after the funeral especially when the calls and visit of comfort to the family left behind become even less then'.

Grief and the mourning stage of process is a very PERSONAL and INDIVIDUALISED process. Some people never ever grieve at all for a departed loved one. There is NO right and wrong WAY for any given person to GRIEVE AT ALL.

I also SAY that there is also NO SLATED grieving TIME FRAME period either. Some folk are lucky enough to be OVER grief in a matter of hours BUT MAJORITY of folk do grieve for MONTHS AND EVEN MANY YEARS.

From the RESEARCH that I have all PERSONALLY DONE on the topic of GRIEF grieving for months and years ISNT wrong, a crime or even a sign of a severe mental problem to as well.

HERE A LIST OF THINGS NOT AT ALL UNDER ANY CIRCUMSTANCES TO

DON'T EVER SAY OR TELL TO A GRIEVING PERSON:-

1.)   Get over it (not to grieve anymore)

2.)   Stop crying (stop grieving)

3.)   Stop the tears

4.)   Get yourself together

5.)   I forbid you to grieve anymore

6.)   Your banned from grieving at home (forbid grief at home)

7.)   Your banned from grieving at church (forbid grief at church)

8.)   Don't EVER ask the last person with a now deceased person what the person last WORD ALL WAS. (that ALL morbid, cold and heartless)

9.)   Don't EVER tell a grieving person to get a grip

10.)   Don't EVER tell a grieving person that they are selfish

11.)   Don't EVER tell a grieving person that there are other worse of in situations then they all currently are now

12.)   Don't YOU EVER blame a grieving person for some one else's death

13.)   Don't YOU ever FAULT a grieving person for some one else's death either

The BIGGIEST NUMBER ONE NO OF ALL TO EVER DO GO AD SAY TO A IN VERY DEEP EXTREME GRIEVING

PERSON is that is your fault why your loved one is dead or died.

It is NOT the thing to DO OR SAY at all PERIOD. It is the WRONG thing to SAY ever and period. It is ALSO not at ALL the thing to say and speak EVEN to other ALOUD even. You are indeed ASKING for troubles you won't be in control of if YOU keep on saying it TOO.

It is NOT AT ALL THE DONE AND RIGTH THING to keep on saying and telling a VERY DEEPLY GRIEVING person lady or man that at ALL. You are going about IT all in the wrong way.

You CANT take it BACK or unsay what YOU just then chose to SAY once you do say it as WELL. You CAN apologise all that you MAY want to AFTER you do say IT but the DAMAGE has ALREADY been done and caused with THOSE there VERY cutting WORDS of yours THERE.

WHEN YOU ARE seeing, talking to and dealing with a GRIEVING person PLEASE do always THINK before you speak and ACT. Folks do use your common sense. REMBER who you are dealing with here a very deeply disturbed along with grieving, mourning, distraught, upset and unhappy person so DO always keep and also bare that ALL in mind too.

LESS is more folks. REMBER to be VERY thoughtful and considerate to all those that are indeed deeply grieving the loss of a LOVED one. Comments like she died 2 weeks ago or 2 months ago are UNHELPFUL.

God alone DOES give and take away when he is ready NOT people. Folks do die in murder, suicide, car crash, bike crash, hit and runs, sickness, illness, plane crash, boat crash, drowning, etc.

You get folk all committing suicide because a death was so expected and UNEXPECTED to all along and around too both. The person left behind snaps and kills themselves of even.

This all isn't to be taken lightly. This is all very serious indeed. Folks NEED TO STOP being and acting CLUELESS when it comes to the WHOLE ENTIRE grieving process and be MORE kind heartened and sympathetic instead too.

Grieving and mourning the lost and death of a loved ONE whether the person gone was A blood relative or not doesn't make the grieving PERSON crazy, mad, a danger to themselves, a danger to others or at ALL sectionable either.

People do DIE all of the time ALL daily, weekly, monthly and yearly all of the time. Folks do need to be careful and watch themselves in BOTH their actions and words to. Do STOP all of the CALLOUS comments to a grieving person that folk keep on carrying on with.

The comments are just SO heartless and cold. Like even an ANIMAL deserves BETTER treatment, understanding, love, companionship and sympathy SO TO DO GRIEVING PEOPLE LIKE AND AS ME TOO.

NO ONE person ACTION, REACTION AND TAKE ON ANY GIVEN DEATH is ever the same as the very next person when all is done and said in the end. Any one that says so is a bold faceted liar too.

You CANT and I repeat cant CHOSE what family line that you all get born into the only thing that you can indeed chose is WHO your friends ALL are and of course the COMPANY that you all do KEEP.

If folks comments to how your coping and grieving to the loss of a loved one isn't HELPING your recovery PERSONAL GRIEF PROCESS along with if you are OUT RIGTH telling folk how they can help you to COPE better and folk ARE refusing to do as you have ASKED or choosing to ignore your request CUT THAT PERSON off and out of your life for good.

At times YOU on hearing of the death of a loved one want to immediately die too to be with the lost loved one. That feeling is natural to get, have and feel for a time. Don't feel any way about it at all.

Don't EVER feel dirty, unclean or sinful for thinking and feeling it. Just don't try to kill yourself of like I kept all saying and trying to do. Go out and find the RIGTH people to grieve with. It does indeed WORK and HELP when you do so.

Make SURE to choose very WISELY for not any old and young person will *do who TO grieve, confide in and talk to. I KNOW what I'm talking about here. I have experienced this side of things for myself.*

Avoid like the plague ALL negative people in and out of church both family and friends that are around YOU. They will HINDER and not aid you in your process of GRIEF. It MUST be done and so. NOT grieving at all and SHOWING no emotions at all period does you MORE harm than good too.

TRUST ME ON THIS at time you think and believe that all of your tears are done and over but THEN out of the blue you do find that the tears are all still coming and flowing like the death was only just yesterday when in fact it was just months or years ago.

FOR MYSELF PERSONALLY going to the church she went too, seeing the seat where she used to sit at the morning service, flash backs to the funeral by CHOICE AND FORCE OF NASTY PEOPLE, seeing her photograph, hearing a song sung at the funeral and extra ALL continue and still do send me into CRYING SPELLS.

From the research that I done myself grieving by WAY of tears, crying and bawling is indeed a NATURAL and understandable sign and show of GRIEF. It is not at all wrong thing to do and show OTHER when you are in deep grief and GRIEVING.

Peoples got the RIGTH including me to mourn, grieve, cope and deal with it in WHATEVER and HOWEVER way we all DO see fit to do so all IN. NO ONE IN THE UK AND WORLDWIDE no MATTER who the PERSON is has got the RIGTH to tell a grieving PERSON NOT to bawl, NOT to show emotion and NOT to show upset at the other person death either.

How folk do feel is all part of a process known as the GRIEVING PROCESS readers. At times you cry and other times your fine and don't. Daily you can't sleep. Daily you can't eat.

You get these chest pains. You get these headaches. You can't at all cope with life anymore.

At time you don't want to get out of bed at all period. You throw up at time what you eat because you don't really want to eat. That the hard and cold fact of GRIEF folk which is great and severe both.

You feel like a rug has been yanked out from right on under you. You no longer feel involved, together, well, at all happy within yourself, strengthened and okay too.

You just always feel like you are standing in the middle of quick sand and there is no life preserver at all there for you anywhere anymore. You also feel so very much like a ship without a sale.

You do also feel like you have LOST your cover, strength and shield all in one. FOLKS please use the common sense and WISDOM that god gave to you and STOP upsetting grieving folk in WORDS.

It's so not of GOD the comments that folks keep on seeing fit to speak and say to THOSE in grief. Another THING readers is it ISNT at ALL wrong, bad and morbid for a GRIEVING person to REGULARLY visit the grave plait of their dearly departed loved one at all.

We are all in bad and serious time now. This is my story. Nothing special at all but just only my very own story none the less that I am all sharing a little bit of in here. I have had folks that I do know including my granny last year die on me.

This particular lady though I was closer WITH. I called her MUM for she was like more than LIKE a SECOND MUM to me for many years. We were not at all related by blood. It was a SPIRITUAL mom and daughter relationship that we had for the last 14 and halve years.

She and another lady introduced me to the church I go to in 2000. I did not always PLEASE her and the other lady in certain things that I chose to do and say in and out of church both BUT their love and interest in me ALWAYS STAID AND REMAINED THE SAME WITH ME ANYWAY.

She called me the following names: - daughter, niece, handbag and wedderburn when introducing me around to others in and out of church. She supported me at every BIRTHDAY celebration.

She was a STEADY and CONSTANT fixture in my life ALWAYS there TO back, support and help me IN those 14 and a halve years to. SHE NEVER EVER DISAPPOINTED ME and let me down.

She came to all things and events I had going ON including my VERY first book launch. What you saw was always what you got with HER anyway.

She supported you when you were in the RIGTH and when you were in the wrong she didn't. You always knew when she was both happy and unhappy with you. It all did show itself up all on and by her all very fast and quick every single time indeed.

My sole REGRET was that I didn't always treat her right those entire 14 and a halve years that I had her with me. I was rude, disrespectful and hurtful. She always FORGAVE me. She said what she had to say and that was IT.

She IGNORED the other that kept on telling her as she made it a point to tell me to drop me and have nothing more to do with me as they no longer do. She never did as they had said to do EVER.

I could always COUNT on her love no matter what. She took me places with her and paid for me to go places. Once or twice she washed my hair and plaited it for me. She had a beautiful SMILE that lit up ALL places and rooms where she was.

She knew how to dress as well. She was stunning TIMES ten in her outfits, *hats, bags and shoes. A woman TOO all of and after god own HEART. She was REAL AND TRUE. She always did and said what she promised to DO.*

She HELPED many folks all the time in WHATEVER way THAT she ALL could even if it WAS with the LAST of WHAT she HAD too. That all was how and what she was made to be, do and act by god above alone. I THANK GOD FOR HER LIFE AND LEGACY OF REALNESS THAT REMAINS BEHIND TODAY.

When a person is DEEP in grief and distraught do ALWAYS handle the DEEPLY GRIEVING person with extreme care and kiddie gloves TOO. Don't ever just SHOOT of the mouth to a grieving person. THINK.

APPROPRIATE ACTIONS AND WORDS TO A GRIEVING PERSON:-

1.) *A hug*

2.) *Kiss*

3.) *Cuddle*

4.) *Smile*

5.) *Prayer*

6.) *Robbing of back, face and shoulder if person is crying*

7.) *An encouraging word of comfort*

8.) *Inviting person that very day including Sunday to your home for dinner or dinner in the week whichever is sooner*

9.)   *A checking up on the person text*

10.)   *A checking up on the person call*

11.)   *Being a good listening ear to person to talk to if choses to do so*

12.)   *Having the person sleep by you at your home for a night or two*

If YOU are SO clueless YOU are UNABLE to DO any of the ABOVE listed things for the GOOD of a grieving person THEN do GRIEVING people that INCLUDES myself a big and TREMENDOUS favour in all both DOING and SAYING nothing to the GRIEVING people AT all. Everyone is DIFFERENT and not the SAME. We may all look similar but in actuality are ALL very DIFFERENT.

It is so very true that we all got to go at some point in time BUT AND I DO REPEAT HERE BUT YET AGAIN use common SENSE folk HERE instead of being CRUEL and HEARTLESS indeed inside and out to the deeply GRIEVING person which INCLUDES me and SIMPLELY DON'T TELL A DEEPLY GRIEVING PERSON THAT THERE AT ALL. It is just so very indeed WRONG to do to the person. What GOES around always does come AROUND. We all have to go through IT.

It is ALWAYS best and better to always ear and lean on the SIDE of total CAUTION then going and running of your MOUTH without complicating the consequences of doing so FIRST on and to anything and anyone else.

DON'T EVER ADMIT to anyone if you happen to be with SOMEONE that takes ill, collapses, is rushed to the hospital on you or dies when you were near and far from the area there.

LESS is indeed more. Don't at all answer people question of what do you know and what happened either. Also DON'T voluntarily give out information to anyone that does pointedly ask you for IT. Keep your mouth SHOT.

If you DON'T you will solely and greatly regret it indeed and in fact too trust me. Folk will turn on you IM SPEAKING ON EXEPERIENCE here FOLKS and torment you with all that you had talked and shared with them driving you to the point of insanity.

That was all INDEED done to me from the time that a lady like a second mom to me died on the 22 January to her burial on the 25 February and right up to even now.

A BIG SHOT OUT to the following folk for the MASSIVE SUPPORT from my church. MY FEW BLESSINGS:- REVEREND MA HEATHER DIXON, MARIE, MA HENRY, MA ROSLYN,

LYSTRA, JACKIE(GUY ONE), PASTOR FREDDIEE BROWN AND WIFE PAULETTE, MRS VERONA WRIGTH, AUNTIE JULIUS, AUNTIE HAZEL, BISHOP POWELL AND WIFE MARCELLE, AUNT ELSADA, SISTER LUCILLE, RITA, REVEREND NOEL BROWN, THE HALLS, AUNTIE IONIE, NESHALLA, PATRICIA, AYESHA, KERISHA AND THE BLACKS . THANKS FOR LOVE, CARE, HELP, CALLS, TEXTS, HUGS, LISTENING EAR, MONEY, FOOD, DINNER AT YOUR HOMES, CLOTHES, ENCOURAGING WORD AND YOUR GODLYNESS TOWARDS ME TOO AS WELL FROM HER MY LATE MA THELMA HOSPILIZATION ON THE 4 JANUARY TO HER DEATH ON THE 22 JANUARY TO HER BURIAL ON 25

FEBRUARY AND UP TO NOW. THANKS A THOUSAND TIME THANKS. GOD DO BLESS AND KEEP YOU ALL AS YOU DO HIS WILL AND WORK.AMEN.

It turned out for me anyway to be the worst thing possible for it to be found out that it wasn't me that had called the ambulance to the house for my second mom but another church lady who had done it.

I was TOLD all to my face MAINLY and later text messages that it is my fault that my second mom had died because it wasn't I that had called the ambulance to the house for her.

That by me not calling the ambulance to her at the house right away that I had all lost and caused her valuable medical treatment time at the hospital. So many people began telling me that there in and out of church. I do believe it my fault up to now.

One of her sons said that by me raising the alarm that I gave them hope she may make it for 2 week. One of her son called me a hero. Another son told someone over the phone in front of me that if it hadn't been for me that their mom would have been found collapsed and dead in the house later on in that there week or day.

So he was glad that she wasn't alone and that I was with her. Inspite of folk singing my praises I keep replaying the happenings of 4 of January in my head over and over again. I keep on thinking that I did call and text the wrong people for help and advice on that bad day.

When I have repeated to other the bad comments of blame on me folk have said no one should be saying such things to me. The oldest son said several time to me to send folk saying it to him and he will sort them out.

One of her best friend when I told her said that I done the best that I could for her at the time and take comfort in knowing that. Another of my aunt best friends said that I was there for her when she needed me the most which was all very good indeed.

Another church member said when I told her that I was being blamed for her death that how I had saved her life by calling the other church lady that called the ambulance and that how I could have made excuses and not gone when the son had texted me to come to the house.

Another church member told me that I DID DO REAL GOOD and also that I am not in charge of who lives and dies only god is. People stab you AT times in the heart and back.

People will always talk whether what you did and said was good or bad for that how people all are and always will be too. We are not in control of none of that there at all period. People NEED to seriously THINK before they do and say anything at all.

Ask yourself this question first me too would god himself be pleased if I did say this? Would god do this? Would god be pleased if I said and done this to so and so?

I MYSELF greatly struggle in doing and saying right over wrong things to in here having more failures at it then I DO successes at it. BUT AND AGAIN I DO SAY BUT life is a learning curve.

We all REGARDLESS of name, age, title, status, schooling and back ground got LIFES many lessons to LEARN by error usually in the world and culture of today that none of us are able to escape. It will EITHER make or break you these life LESSONS here.

No one KNOWS it all all of the TIME. Our lessons, strengths and testimonies of victory are all THERE to uplift and encourage others on what we overcame so they can all do so TOO. We are ALL affected by a death IN one way, shape and form ALL regardless of what the dead person WAS and MEANT to us.

SOME FOLK HIDE THEIR GRIEF WELL. Majority of us do WEAR our GRIEF and sorrow on our faces and sleeves too all *around to be SEEN BY all. THERES NO ONE ALIVE LEFT THAT ISNT.*

It does SHOW the CALLOUSNESS of the people in the world of TODAY it does when THEY KICK YOU WHEN YOU ARE at your lowest of low down and GRIEVING the loss of a loved one regardless of IF the person dead was YOUR relative or only just a friend. It all so very bad and wrong it all is too.

What happens to people I do ask? Why are some people just so heartless and cold to other people who are in extreme and severe GRIEF too? It all just so very sad indeed to all do watch, see, hear and behold all around too.

People GRIEVING all just need to do and just hang onto the following things here:-

1.) *God*
2.) *Fellow mourners*
3.) *Fellow grievers*
4.) *Their faith in god (believe me you will be tried, tested and whipped by other)*
5.) *Keep all of the cherished memories you have of departed loved one all close to your HEART AND HAND always*

THOSE PERSONS UNENDING LEGACY LIVES ON IN THEIR BLOOD RELATIVES, FFIENDS, POSSESSTIONS LEFT BEHIND, YOU AND ME TOO!!!!!AMEN.

In a tragedy that eventually leads to the death both expected and MAINLY unexpected of a LOVED one you do find out all BOTH fast and quick YOU DO whose REALLY for you along with not for you, the fake people around you from the REAL people coming around you, whose REALLY got your front and back covered along with who doesn't and also ALONG with YOUR friends from your enemies.

You do ALSO see, hear, know and realise for YOURSELF that all really on is HOW cheap TALK of other chatting to and around you really ON is as well TOO. When you are in TRADEGY, MOURNING AND IN DEEP HEAVY

GRIEF nothing but ACTION doers will do for being NEXT to and around YOU at that point there in time.

IT'S THE DOERS to help and assist you that will all COUNT and matter to YOU when you are DEALING with BOTH a TRADEGY and a DEATH.YOU also finally start seeing folk FINALLY for WHO and what they really on ARE as WELL too. You then get a REALITY check on a MAJOR scale regarding how really UNREAL most FOLKS are along with CAN be all AROUND, beside and NEXT to you too when you are in and DEALING with a TRADEGY and DEATH whether expected or unexpected in

YOUR life AT any given point in time there of a set year TOO as well.

It does ALL do TRUST me at times CAUSES your heart to ALL stop and give you as well this CAUSE for pause moment on top. You see and realise for YOURSELF that GENERALLY the majority of the FOLKS are not at ALL as and what they ALL say and also do CLAIM to all be at ALL. With that THERE knowledge, disappointment, let down and rejection that DOES come YOUR way at that there most critical POINT in time.it MAKES you at that POINT question BOTH god and your faith at that there TIME.

When BOTH a death and tragedy HAPPENS in your life it usually meant TO draw and bring the PEOPLE it ALL does CONCERN all closer and nearer together NORMALLY but more often than NOT IT ALL DOESN'T. There in fighting that happens INSTEAD over the funeral arrangements, the will if any at all exists, who gets the inheritance first, who gets the inheritance last and ALSO on who is to get what TOO.

It is ALL very bad and sad indeed OVERALL. With all of that drama and confusion that follows a PERSON death it UNFORTUNATELY drives wedges, distances and upsets between some

FOLKS permanently. All of a SUDDEN and just like THAT out of the BLUE you all start hearing FROM and seeing folk less and less. FOLK change and turn on YOU all picking and refusing to when to RESPOND to if at all ever PERIOD any calls and text messages that you do ALL happen to send to THEM.

On other side of THINGS here those that you had thought that you KNEW oh so VERY well get ALL funny and weird on you to as well ALL of a SUDDEN to THERE too. It then BECOME a thing of YOU see me today BUT not tomorrow you DON'T scene and situation TOO going on. AGAIN you realise YOU don't really KNOW *someone at all that you had truly THOUGHT that you had known for MANY years AND see their REAL and TRUE side and nature all ONLY just then and now.*

IT'S all just VERY devastating it all. When money and estate enter the EQUATION you do see a whole NEW different side and stance of CERTAIN people. Cover ups occur and take place because OF it. You also REALISE that the person that you had thought that YOU knew for MANY years AIENT really your friend AND company at ALL and NEVER really was EITHER. It all just YOUR reality CHECK and WAKE up

CALL to how things are and go from NOW onwards too.

You SEE and know for yourself that THIS was indeed ALL about pretence on a VERY high level, pretend, fakeness and camouflage TOO acting JUST because the person all COULD do so and that with you. SECRETS long AGO hidden suddenly ALL crops and pop up NOW all over the place just coming up and to life ALL here and there WITH the unexpected DEATH and tragedy that does come and all DOES happen with AN unexpected death and tragedy loss of loved one REGARDLESS of whether a relative of your or a friend just then and like that PERIOD.

It BREAKS hearts it does AND shatters souls in the left behind AFTERMATH of it all TOO. You then all REALISE at that point and stage in the GAME of life more and more THAT all is too that you REALLY on got no one at ALL anymore and also TTHAT it is REALLY just you against the WORLD. What is DONE in the DARK will also so TOO always come TO the light.

It is ALL like the people in the world of TODAY do snap, go mad, go crazy and JUST do totally lose it in the FACE of both a tragedy and a death both. I PERSONALLY don't KNOW which one is indeed WORSE and EASIER to all BOTH take and handle. An EXPECTED death or an **UNEXPECTED** death **REALLY** when you really do look and evaluate it all there in front and center of your **FACE** and **LIFE** both as it all is to be. For and to me **BOTH** are as bad as the other.

If you know someone is **DYEING** from say cancer, heart disease or aids you are told the death is to happen in x amount of weeks , months or even years so you can all **PREPARE** and try to get **USE** to the person being gone for **GOOD** from your life from **THEN**. So for **EXAMPLE** at least you can **MAKE** **PEACE** if you have too, say **SORRY** if it something due to the person, take person on a trip somewhere, spend

EXTRA quality time with the person for the remaining time with them and MAKE SURE you with them when they breathe their last BREATHE.

Unexpected death is just so very DIFFERENT indeed. One minute the person is WITH you and the next the person is JUST gone. There no warning. There is just nothing REALLY. You just GET a call, text or email that so and so is GONE from someone else. We live in a cold world for sure. I recall a family complaining and being in HEARTACHE break. Their ONLY son was killed in a car accident abroad on holiday with friends.

Before THE police could contact and inform them of the death ONE of the daughters was sent a Facebook notification saying that he HAD been killed and that the family has the person condolences. For ME that was cold, heartless and unfeeling. The FIRST way how the family heard of the DEATH was an INPERSONAL Facebook message on a computer that was clearly VIEWED and seen by OTHER so NOT only by them the actual family as well.

The daughter then informed the passing of their son death WELL before the police came and told them of IT as a result of it all. That WAS so wrong that there was on many LEVELS.I heard another STORY of a SHOCKING death. Do bear in mind this was over 5 years ago. I hence can't recall if the pastor wife that died was talking to her pastor hubby or the couple only child in the kitchen of the house. She was talking to one of them.

She was about to say something else when she just suddenly DROPPED to the ground in front of them JUST like that. Something clearly happened that made them REALISE that she was ACTUALLY dead on the kitchen floor there JUST like that in front of them. I attended that funeral. It was JUST so very sad INDEED. The lady HADNT ever been sick a day in her entire life time ever and at all PERIOD. She was just 50 years old.

DEATH is no RESPECTOR of age. TOMMORROW AIENT PROMISED. I REPEAT again to you my readers here folks that TOMMOROW ISNT PROMISED TO ANYONE. Do PLEASE always WATCH and CHECK yourself. HERE today and gone tomorrow. I REPEAT again HERE today and gone tomorrow. Ask yourself would god do that? Would god say this? If someone said this to me how would I like it?.

If someone did this to me how would I like it? Am I a forgiving person? Do I hold things against others? Am I a humble person? Pride does come before a fall? If I died TODAY is THERE anything current or past THAT I done or said pertaining to OTHER I see all the time THAT would cause god NOT to allow me up THERE with him in HEAVEN? Watch out! Again I say watch out! Do you betray folk confidence? Check YOURSELF over!

Folk DO deal and cope with the loss of a LOVED one in the worse of ways possible at TIME here. Your mind, body, heart and soul CANT seem to COPE and HANDLE at all WHAT your hearing, seeing, being told and informed about at that THERE set and given time pertaining to a death

ANNOUNCEMENT at time. It DOESN'T seem real. It JUST all too much to TAKE in, see, deal with and do at that there TIME indeed overall.

People do NEED to rember WHO they are all talking to when they are INDEED talking and ALSO know what their PLACE all is too as well on top. Take the HINTS that a DEEPLY GRIEVING person give you to BACK OFF, DON'T COME NEAR AND QUITE PLAINLY TO JUST SIMPLELY STAY AWAY from them so JUST be gone.

BE smart and intelligent all ENOUGH to by process of both fast and quick ELIMINATION know ALL for and within THEMSELVES when it is the

WRONG time to speak and SAY something to a DEEPLY GRIEVING person and to also always know when the RIGTH time to speak all is too on top as well. At TIME the BEST thing is to ABSOLUTELY say NOTHING at all to a DEEPLY GRIEVING person for a HUG is WORTH a THOUSAND along with a MILLION words INSTEAD.

A hug is the BEST, SAFEST AND SURIEST thing to DO always and without a DOUBT if in a query and at a loss of words for the right thing to SAY to a DEEPLY GRIEVING PERSON.

THINK people THINK. the TIME and day RIGTH after a FUNERAL to a MAXIMUM of 10 months after a DEAD person burial and funeral is a *FRAGILE, TOUCHY, FRESH AND PAINFUL* time indeed all around for *THOSE* deeply *GRIEVING* and *LEFT BEHIND* folk so do *LEAVE* your *BRAINLESS, TACTLESS AND CLUELESS* comment *OF* it time to get over it now out of the conversation.

I am saying this on *BEHALVE* of all *DEEPLY GRIEVING PEOPLE LIKE ME FOR THESE* comments are *NOT* at all wanted by the *CAUGTH* hearer and just *QUITE SIMPLELY* need leaving to be said to the person all 3 years and *MORE* after the *GONE* person funeral and burial too. *YOUR SILENCE* on this is very much *APPREICIATED*.

CONCLUSION

Church leaders are all flesh and blood folk like us. They aren't perfect or saint. Do always must do rember that there to. They AIENT god either. We all have to AND must DO respect them ALL in their roles as either a BISHOP, SENOIR PASTOR, FIRST LADY, PASTOR, PASTOR WIFE, ASSISTANT PASTOR, REVEREND, MINISTER, EVANGELIST, JUNIOR MINISTER, DEACON, DEACONESS, HEAD OF DEPARTMENT AND ELDER but DON'T you ever worship and idolise them.

They sacrifice TIME at home to do all that they do at church. Not all Church leaders and department heads are paid wages to live by their respective churches too. It ISNT easy what they all do and say for us all. THEY CANT PLEASE US ALL OF THE TIME IN THE CHURCH DECISIONS THAT THEY DO ALL HAVE TO MAKE AT TIMES. They need OUR prayers and not OUR moaning complaints.

They all do so at time preach, moderate services, introduce speakers, teach, host events, do weddings, do funerals, do christenings, visit those sick at home, visit those sit in hospitals, and do baptisms. More often than not church leaders along with church office staff workers and department heads ARE NOT thanked for all that they do upfront and behind the scenes BOTH in and out of church. I DO THANK THEM ALL THOUGH NOW.

I do so truly BELIEVE that THEY are all chosen by GOD. That god HAND is over, on and upon them. At TIMES church leaders and department heads do STUMBLE AND FALL. Don't hold it AGAINST them when they do so. It ONLY shows that they are HUMAN just like we untitled folk are. PRAY ALWAYS FOR THEM TO ARISE AGAIN. It so NEEDED in the day and time that we are all living in at this here time.

I know that under god leading that they all WILL continue to work well together in unity, pray and lead THEIR *respective churches in the straight and narrow way of the lord to the best of their ABILITY as they have done thus far in the X amount of years CHURCH LEADING AND DEPARTMENT heading for in their RESPECTIVE church.*

I am a NOBODY of significance or importance. I got NO title after my NAME of mbe, cbe, dame and knight either. My only claim to ROYALTY folk is that my GOD is a well KNOWN saviour and KING. I am USED TO being mainly ignored and over looked in all things and ways. That changed a LITTLE BIT after my second mom died UNEXPECTEDLY this year here.

People will be SHOCKED at the certain things that you DO notice and see a lot of WHEN you are much UNSEEN and hence you do hear thing that other WON'T ever hear too as WELL.I got a lot to say though. Folk CAN take it or leave it. For ME GOD ISNT AT all CURRENTLY pleased with what going on world-wide both in and out of church.

I have been shocked in my RECENT DISCUSSION with various folk that all do agree with my thought and ENCOURAGED me to include my train of thoughts on these TOUCHY matters in my GRIEF PROCESS book here. We all KEEP on hearing in THE newspaper, television and radio of these crises of disaster ALL WORLDWIDE AND not just only here in the UK.

God is NOT playing with NOBODY. God does mean SERIOUS business here. He is SHOWING his anger. There is a VERY HIGH level of disobedience going on in the UK churches ESPECIALLY as well as worldwide TOO as WELL. God, your bishop, your pastor or minister has SPECIFICAILLY spoken to certain FOLK telling them to STEP DOWN and remove themselves from certain church department, role and duties ALL ages ago EITHER permanently or temporarily.

These folks have not stepped down from and left these posts of theirs as of YET all up to now and TODAY. God says as LONG as you stay in the ROLE that he and other HAVE told you to step away from and vacate YOU WILL REMAIN OUT OF ALIGHNMENT AND POSITION.YOU WILL BE STAGMENT AND NOT GROW! Move AND move NOW.

There is a high level of LACK of fearing of god in the house of the lord. God ISNT PLEASED BY THIS HERE AT ALL. I REPEAT THAT GOD isn't pleased at all by this. We need to get BACK to that there place that we all have somehow come away FROM where we

FEAR god ABOVE all AND anything ELSE!

There a LACK of holiness in the house of the lord in the UK and also worldwide. The lord is VERY displeased by this all indeed. It an ANYTHING GOES ATMOSPHERE these days here thing occurring. It is so WRONG. He wants a purpose filling crowd of a CHURCH. Many want to lead AND none want to follow. Many ARE willing but the WORKERS are just still so very few.

There is an INCREASE of gay folk being EXPOSED in churches. That there is definitely NOT OF GOD what is going on there anyway. If you GIVE access into 1 the masses will COME!!! There is an INCREASE of folks leading a service or moderating WITHOUT praying first. God ISNT PLEASED BY THIS AT ALL. Prayer should ALWAYS be DONE first before you get up on any PALLPIT to do something WHETHER in UK or abroad. Prayer is your COVER AND SHIELD.

This goes FOR as well praise and worship singers, preachers and prayer givers on a Sunday morning as well all too. Getting on the pall pit to do something without having prayed first is indeed a very big ABOMINATION that all it there. Praying beforehand is so very KEY thing to do indeed to enable you personally to truly do

SHAKE OF ALL AND any undue stress, badness and extera that may be hanging around you. You are meant to be ushering in god spirit there.

Holiness at SOME of the churches worldwide has gone right out of the WINDOW all totally and completely now TOO. Lord please do have mercy on MY and other folk SOUL.

1.) Would you ever leave your home without your house key with you?

2.) Would you ever leave your house for a trip without your passport?

3.) Would you leave your house without keys to your car to drive to work in?

4.) Would you leave home without your travel card?

5.) Would you leave home without your oyster card?

6.) Would you go to church without your bible?

No, no, no, no, no and no is the answer. The SAME policy should be ALWAYS applied to church business as well there. No one SHOULD step out and onto THE pall pit and alter UNTIL THEY HAVE all unburdened and cleansed themselves by PRAYER all first and foremost it is as SIMPLE as that.

I no idea how many readers will EITHER agree or disagree with me on this HERE. We need TO get back to THAT there way of knowing RIGTH from wrong all FOR and within OURSELVES. We also NEED to KICK out permanently the world in churches that we let so WILLINGLY in.

We need TO get back to THAT there place of HONEST, REAL and TRUE holiness to our GOD above all and anything ELSE. Do trust and believe that GOD can indeed tell and notice the difference. We need TO get back to THAT there place where we aient AFRAID to throw out the window the SET usual program on a SUNDAY morning and let GOD DO HIS THING, WORK AND MOVE as he WANTS to.

JUST FREE WORSHIP AND LET GOD REIGHN. There a LACK of reverence in the house of the lord in the way how that members DO all do SO talk to, speak to and address their church ministers and leaders all to as WELL. Some of the ways that I DO hear church members ALL addressing and speaking to their pastor I say a quick prayer for the person soul for they know NOT WHAT they all do say.

The place where I was raised was Bermuda ALTHOUGH I was born here in the UK. In the church where I WAS raised up to a church member couldn't enter a pastor office unless you knocked first on the door then Okayed to enter or was invited in. Also THERE would be major trouble if you interrupted a conversation that the said pastor was in already with another person OVER the phone or face to face too.

Bermuda churches are SO very different to UK churches. In UK churches it JUST any old thing will do and go saga NOT all of the time but SOME of the TIME. Both to and for me along with the other that I have been talking to as well in recent weeks THIS IS INDEED the end days and times all HERE and now.

I was bothered and concerned really on I WAS to hear along SIDE many other of the KIPNAPPING and taking of those 200 girls in that African country last year. What A very sad and wicked world THAT we are indeed living in TODAY. You REALLY aren't safe anywhere anymore indeed in this world OF today here. It is all just sad that there.

I was informed and also have done research and heard that a few DID manage to escape BUT the vast majority remain held AGAINST their will there and that even MORE girls got taken yet again LATER on. That ALL barbaric to and for me ANYWAY. My heart DOES bleed very badly and tremendously INDEED for the kidnapped girls families to as well. I pray FOR comfort at this hideous TIME for them all there and to right on NOW. Do PRAY steady for the KIDNAPPED girls and distressed families.

ANOTHER very disturbing happening all to me was the DISAPPEARANCE of that THERE plane in MID AIR over water with over 150 plus folk on-board along with staff in March of 2014.My lord have MERCY. We at the writing of my book here are in April of 2015 and still no one can find that there PLANE. We need the

LORD. My LORD. My lords please do have mercy I BEG on every body's heart and soul right NOW I do ask.

The plane and people REMAIN missing at large too. It DOES greatly concern me even if it doesn't CONCERN anybody ELSE at that there entire plane still has NOT been FOUND yet. Planes that size DON'T just vanish just like that THERE. This is INDEED and truly just a weird ANOLONY. It is ALSO UNHEARD of this all is. On and of you do hear stories of GUESSES of where some folks ALL believe that plane all is TO.

Some say it was shot down, high jacked, electrical charge to it cost it to combust in mid-air, was taken by aliens, is being held for ransom in another country and is so deep underneath the sea it can't be found at all. What I think happened to the plane FOLK don't believe and calling it my delusions. I think god took it in the RAPTURE.

Those that DISAGREE with my belief do PLEASE turn around and tell me where the plane is then. Time will EVENTUALLY tell WHO is right and wrong in their guesses on where the missing plane all is THAT for SURE. All that I can say is god DO help the families without any ANSWERS left behind. No funeral and memorials can

BE done for NO one has any bodies yet to do anything with. IT is all very sad indeed this IS. They REMAIN in limbo still up to NOW. They CAN'T grieve or be happy EITHER for know nothing.

I challenge you reader of my book with these pointed questions here? I am not at all judging you. Of late I am just judging myself and my VERY own slated faults and imperfections. I recall an OLD TIME SAYING TOLD when growing up. If you POINT a finger at someone ELSE always do REMBER that there ALWAYS 10 fingers pointing back at you.

1.) How many folks are starving in churches?

2.) How many folk got no money to live on?

3.) How many folk are on suicide watches?

4.) How many folk are taking anti-depressants in private?

5.) How many folk are starving so that their kids can all eat and drink? MY LORD MY LORD!!

At TIMES you GET more help FROM none church members and goers then ACTUAL church members and goers. OTHER times church member help you OUT more than none church member do. I AM NUMBER ONE GUILTER OF THIS. At times due to bad situations MY OWN FAULT AS WELL AS BEYOND

MY CONTROL LIKE WHEN IM ROBBED OF MY MONEY OR PAYING DEBTS OF I am taking from folk on and off INSTEAD of giving to folks back.

1.) When will the double standards go?

2.) When will the gossiping stop and go too?

3.) When will the back biting stop?

4.) When will the character assassination of an innocent person good name end?

5.) When will smear campaign stop? MY LORD MY LORD!!

6.) When will showing blatant favouritism of one person over the next be stopped once and for all too?

7.) When will churches get rid of clicks and groupings in church?

You hear someone needs money. U give to the PERSON discreetly saying god BLESS you and slip a £10 or so on INTO the person hand asking for the lord to TRIPLE what they just got by you.

You hear that a church brethren is homeless and sleeping on the streets. U get the person of the streets and into your very own home until the person is back on their feet once again.

You hear of a person starving. You offer to take the person grocery shopping OR go get the person shopping DISCREETLY and drop it outside where the person lives with the person name on it.

You're in a shop getting yourself something. You hear that a church brethren is short on their bill say 50p. You pay it and keep it to YOURSELF what you did just do. You see a church brethren needs their hair done quite urgently. Instead of telling the person that their hair stinks really badly you take the person home with you, feed them and wash their hair for them afterwards.

A church person asks you for a lift home. You take the person home NOT asking for gas money even though the person lives quite a distance away from you for it is the godly thing to DO. Here a part of my history and biography. Being BLANKED AND SNOBBED by other ALL of the time HURTS just as REJECTION hurts.

I will ALWAYS hence make friends with folks that ARE being treated like that by others TOO. These MISUNDERSTOOD folk like me have my HEART, PRAYERS AND THOUGHTS. I henceforth will always be on their side as WELL in controversies.

I'm a FIGTHER for the UNDERDOGS in and out of church ALL as and like ME. I have been homeless and slept on the streets on and off for many years. MOST time it my own fault for not paying rent and hence forth the eviction out came to me.

OTHER time I was a victim OF assault, harassment, anti-social behaviour and bullying which lead to me leaving the place I lived ON MY own steam HENCE making myself intentionally HOMELESS 6 time THAT WAS. I hence have a big HEART AND SYMPATHY for ALL homeless and street people having DONE that MYSELF. I speak on EXSPERIENCE here to other now.

I was bullied and teased FROM nursery school, primary school and high school. I was TORTURED because I repeated nursery school THANKS to my mom and hence was called mentally retarded and insane from the age of 3 years old. THINGS LIKE that NEVER ever leave you.

It is why I ACT the way I do in life trials and tribulations and am HOW I am in troubles to as well. I am sure that NONE of my READERS here had folk take gum out of their mouths and put it in YOUR hair. Then your mom had to CUT gum out leaving you WALKING around place with PATCHES in head for months on END.

I'm also sure that NONE of my readers had folks DUMP trash bins full of DIRT AND TRASH over your very HEAD and CALLING you dirty smelly *and ugly trash afterwards. This is some of my LIFE experiences READERS. Not PLEASANT and not NICE at all.*

What you DO for other asked for and not asked for NEEDS to stay between you and that there person and NOT be shared with OTHER for EITHER recognition, reward or acknowledgement. WE NEED TO BE REAL. We NEED TO BE REAL. That is ALL gone, lacking and missing at ALL churches around the world by BOTH church goers and none church goers to.

WHY DOES MY MONEY NEVER LAST ME FOR THE TIME THAT IT SHOULD DO? I'm EITHER paying A business, company or person back court ordered debts, I was robbed of my money, I paying back lent money, I paying back old debts, I paying back new debts, I collapsed and accidentally broke something in a shop that I must pay for now and paying of rent arrears.

I forgot my photo id card and had to pay a penalty charge to the ticket inspector folk and quite often I am walking the streets and see homeless folks there that BREAK my heart to BITS and I WITHOUT thinking wind out blessing them on and off between £10 to £280 depending on what other things I have to pay on and off on that particular week.

I HAVE A THING FOR HOMELESS,VULNERABLE, IGNORED, ROUGH SLEEPING FOLK, FOLKS DELIBERATELY EXCLUDED FROM THINGS AT CHURCH AND SCHOOL BY OTHERS, FOLKS DELIBERATELY LEFT OF GUEST LISTS FOR PARTIES -WEDDINGS -RECEPTIONS AS WELL AS CHRISTENING CELEBRATIONS AND ALWAYS WILL DO SO TOO. ALL OF THOSE THINGS IS ME INSIDE AND OUT ALL OF THE TIME AT CHURCH AND OTHER EVENTS.

TOO many time to count in my YEARS living here I BEEN in that position TOO. I KNOW what it all GIVES. You have wants and needs that *you are relying on other to HELP you to meet. Because your PROBLEMS are REPEATATIVE and EVERY week FOLKS that are related to and know you LOSE patience with you NOT taking their advices, accuse you of loving the position you are in, tell you off because the problems keep on happening to you all of the time and say god helps those that help themselves so they hence forth not helping you in ANY way, shape or form anymore.*

I will always GIVE to homeless and street folks even if it's the last of what I got and have for the NEXT 3 to 2 weeks. God ALWAYS provides someone to give me it back to me.

MOST times I DON'T have to repay what other give me back. Other TIMES I been BLESSED to find money on the ground, in shops and on 2 occasions money sticking out of a cash machine when I been in DIRE need.

ONE OF MY LONG REIGN DREAM OF DREAMS IS TO GET A LARGE SUM OF MONEY FROM SOME PLACE OR SOMEONE AND GET ALL OF THE CURRENT MEN, LADIES, ELDERLY FOLKS, DISABLED FOLKS AND KIDS ALL CURRENTLY SLEEPING ROUGH ON THE ROADS, STREETS AND PARK BENCHS OF THE STREET FOR GOOD.GOD ALWAYS GIVES US OUT HEARTS DESIRES AND I KNOW THAT WISH OF

MINE WILL COME TO PASS WHEN THE SEASON AND TIMING IS RIGTH.

There should be ABSOLUTELY no one sleeping rough in this here country of the LONDON UK here nowhere. We are all ABOVE this bad pattern already. I WILL AT SOME STAGE BE A MAJOR ROLE AND KEY PLAYER USED BY GOD TO END THE PLIGTH OF POORNESS AND POVERTY IN THE UK AND ABROAD too IN THE PRECIOUS NAME OF JESUS REAL SOON TO AS WELL. there is a book that is LONG OVERDUE to that I WILL release on the MISUNDERSTOOD HOMELESS folk in the UK here at some point in time if GOD DOES SPEAR MY LIFE TOO. This is a topic NEAR AND DEAR to my heart too.

I have so VERY MANY dreams people. I have SO many VISIONS that I BELIEVE are sent by god to me of CALMNESS, PEACE, EASE, HAPPINESS, SUCCESS, ENDING OF ALL THE WARS, ENDING OF ALL THE FIGHTING, ENDING OF ALL THE KILLING, ENDING OF ALL THE DOMESTIC VIOLENCE, ENDING OF ALL COUNTRIES HOMELESSNESS WORLD WIDE NOT JUST ONLY HERE IN THE UK, ENDING OF FOLK BEING KILLED BY POLICE IN POLICE CUSTODY THAT ARE GUILTY OF NOTHING OTHER THEN THE VERY COLOUR OF THEIR SKIN AND WE ALL

BEING BUSINESS OWNERS OUTRIGTH IN CHARGE OF OUR VERY OWN MONEY AND HENCEFORTH DESTINY TOO LEAD BY GOD not man.

I know in gods OWN TIME that there CHANGE OF MINE will SO TOO COME. I DON'T know the how and when for I AIENT god but HE does already know IT. We need to get back to those DAYS AND TIMES of REALNESS, being our brothers and sisters KEEPER in BOTH actions and words, not SHARING private texts and emails sent to you WITH others without PERMISSION first and keeping someone CONFIDENCE no matter what and above any and all else too THERE.

If and when those things DO GO AND CHANGE YOU will see all churches packed up and full to OVERFLOW. But as long as churches and more especially CHURCH people keep on doing, saying and behaving as they are NOW then god WONT MOVE and things do stay the same as well. Folk whom I let proof read and go through my book called me a hypocrite, said that the very things I am accusing other of having done to me I am doing now in my book to them, I was called judgemental, told that I would be sued by folks if I publish this here book and so on.

I AM NOT JUDGING OTHER JUST ONLY JUDGING ALONG WITH BEING HARD ON ONLY JUST MYSELF. If other are honest and see themselves in my book here THEN I have DONE my writing JOB here VERY well then in TAKING folk on my writing journey with me and being a PART of positive CHANGE in other people lives. NO one trusts GOD all the time. We all REGARDLESS of age and title got TRUSTING issues for good and bad reasons with BOTH god and other too as well here.

We all ALSO have different TESTS of faith in god in DIFFERENT ways. JUST like with the GRIEF PROCESS no one grief, trust and faith is the SAME because we are all coming from DIFFERENT cultures, backgrounds and educational standing. NO one at all LIFE journey AND battle in THEIR life time span is the SAME regardless of if the other person a relative or friend of yours or not.

I hope that my BOOK touched you in the same way and SPIRIT that it had all did TOUCH ME to all do write it up for you to read. My book a TESTIMONY to the goodness of JESUS our LORD and also that DREAMS FROM YOUR CHILDHOOD CAN STILL COME TRUE AND HAPPEN FOR YOU too. DON'T GIVE IN AND UP. Keep HOPE ALIVE too.

I have myself PERSONALLY let go of ALL of the wrongs that other have indeed done to me FROM birth to now GO. Being BITTER, UNFORGIVING and NEGATIVE bring on SICKNESS and EXTERA your way too.

That there are things that I most DEFINITELY don't want to do, see and be around at all period. I have DONE wrongs to others myself that most TIMES I don't even APPOLOGISE for.

WE ALL from the HIGHIEST BISHOP AT ANY GIVEN CHURCH IN UK AND ABROAD to the YOUNGIEST PERSON at a church have ALL sinned and fallen short of the GLORY OF GOD at least 1 in our life TIME.

THOSE IN CHURCH (AND DO TRUST ME that there are MANY folk like this and that THERE) that claim to have not sinned at LEAST 1 ARE BOLD FACETED liars.

Only god is the PERFECT AND SINLESS one. We all have PASTS. Some are BETTER than other at burying and hiding their VERY colourful pasts.

We ALL HAVE MADE mistakes in our lives and also in the choices that we ALL do make that WE wish we could change and undue BUT we simply CANT.

I know of a WELL known bishop here in the UK who is gay and his wife refuses to leave him. IT'S not at all how MANY sins and how OFTEN that you do fall DOWN.

IT IS ALL IN NOT STAYING DOWN BEATEN AND DEFEATED AT ALL IN THAT SITUATION THAT YOU ARE IN AT THAT THERE TIME.

IT IS IN ARISING AGAIN.

IT IS IN STANDING UPRIGTH AGAIN.

IT IS IN PRIDE GOING AWAY AND FOLKS REMAINING HUMBLE.

IT IS IN FOLK REMBERING WHERE IT ALL IS THAT THEY ALL DID COME FROM ALL TOO AND AS WELL HERE TO.

IT IS IN KNOCKING ON THAT THERE CLOSED DOOR UNTIL IT SWINGS BACK OPEN WIDE TO YOU.

IT IS IN NOT ACCEPTING AND TAKING ANY NO ANSWER ON THING BUT PRESSING ON TO A YES.

I end on this here note dear book readers of mine. THE GRIEVING PROCESS ALL IN AND OUT OF CHURCH is a VERY personalised along with individualised PROCESS that different to us all WHEN it hits us ALL every day of every hour of any skated given time of a SET year .

NO ONE is LEFT unaffected by this GRIEVING PROCESS here I say NO ONE is and those that say that they are not at all affected by the LOST and DEATH of a BELOVED relative or friend is a bold faceted liar and nothing else but that there .

For ALL of us EVEN if we fail to SHOW grief, mourning and upset RIGTH away we WILL eventually given TIME passing onwards do so and just THAT there at some POINT in time later ON. Only god ALONE knows if that LATER on showing grief is months or years LATER.

You DO and WILL miss what you have LOST and that does go for ALL of us people left behind. SOME people are BLESSED to see along with speak to over the phone THEIR relative and friend every day of the week.

For other folks THAT not the case. You ONLY see and speak to that there person on and off. THE CLOSENESS with the now deceased REMAIN regardless of HOW often you may how SEEN and SPOKEN to that person for.

LET US BE REAL HERE. For those folk that are USE to seeing or hearing from now deceased person daily every week YOU will especially MISS that GONE person for the person is NO longer on the other end of the phone to take your call ANY more NOR are they around to come and SEE you NO more.

ONCE that BOND and CONNECTION is made between you and that person it REMAIN intact until you SEE each other again in HEAVEN one day. NO ONE is exempt from that there.

Printed in Great Britain
by Amazon